Lent-Easter Bible Study for Kids 2025

A 40-Day Spiritual Companion

Judah Publishing

Table of Contents

Introduction

Welcome to Your Lent Journey!

Hey there, friend! Are you ready for an amazing adventure? This book is your special guide for the season of Lent—a time when we learn more about Jesus, grow in our faith, and get our hearts ready for Easter.

Lent is like a journey, and every journey needs a good plan. Along the way, you'll read Bible stories, pray, and discover fun ways to learn about God's love. Best of all, you'll find out how much Jesus cares about YOU!

So, grab your Bible, a journal, or a notebook, and let's start this adventure together. Are you ready? Let's go!

What is Lent?

Lent is a special time before Easter when we take 40 days to get closer to God. Think of it like getting ready for a big celebration! Just like we clean our house before a party, Lent helps us clean our hearts so we can celebrate Jesus with joy.

During Lent, many people do three special things:
  ✔ **Pray** – Talk to God and listen to Him.
  ✔ **Fast** – Give up something (like candy or screen time) to focus more on Jesus.
  ✔ **Give** – Help others by sharing, being kind, or doing good deeds.

Lent reminds us of the 40 days Jesus spent in the desert, praying and preparing for His mission (Matthew 4:1-11). It's a time for us to do the same—growing stronger in our faith and making good choices.

So, Lent isn't just about giving up snacks or video games—it's about making room in our hearts for Jesus!

Why Do We Celebrate Easter?

Easter is the BEST news ever! It's when we celebrate that Jesus is alive and that His love is stronger than anything—even death!

Here's why Easter is so important:

🌿 **Good Friday**: Jesus gave His life for us on the cross because He loves us so much.

🌟 **Easter Sunday**: Jesus didn't stay in the tomb—He came back to life! He showed that God's love is more powerful than anything in the world.

Because of Easter, we can have new life in Jesus! It's not just about chocolate eggs and bunnies (though those are fun!). Easter is about hope, love, and the amazing promise that Jesus is always with us.

How to Use This Book

This book is like a map for your Lent journey. Every day, you'll find:

📖 **A Bible Story** – A short passage to help you understand God's love.

🕯 **A Fun Reflection** – A simple way to think about what you read.

⚫ **A Challenge** – Something fun or meaningful you can do.

🙏 **A Prayer** – A way to talk to God.

You can use this book on your own, with a friend, or with your family. It's not about reading fast—it's about spending time with God and growing in your faith.

Are you ready? Let's begin this exciting journey together!

Fun Ways to Learn and Pray

Learning about God and praying doesn't have to be boring! Here are some fun ways to make your Lent journey extra special:

🌀 **Create a Prayer Journal** – Decorate a notebook and write your prayers, thoughts, and Bible verses.

Make a Prayer Corner – Find a cozy spot in your room where you can pray and read the Bible.

Sing Worship Songs – Dance, sing, and praise God with music.

Write Kindness Notes – Leave notes of encouragement for family, friends, or even teachers.

Do Secret Acts of Kindness – Help others without telling them—it's like a surprise gift from Jesus!

Bible Verse Challenge – Memorize one Bible verse each week and teach it to someone.

Prayer and learning about Jesus should be fun! Try different ways to connect with God and see what you enjoy the most.

Week 1: Preparing Our Hearts for the Journey

Ash Wednesday (March 5, 2025)

Day 1:Beginning the Journey

📖 **Bible Reading: Joel 2:12-13**

"Return to me with all your heart, with fasting, weeping, and mourning. Rend your heart and not your garments. Return to the Lord your God, for He is gracious and compassionate."

💡 **Reflection: A Fresh Start with God**

Ash Wednesday is the beginning of Lent—a time when we prepare our hearts for Easter. It's like the start of a long journey where we take time to pray, reflect, and draw closer to Jesus.

The ashes placed on people's foreheads in church remind us that life on Earth is short, but God's love lasts forever. It's not about looking sad or doing things just because we have to. God wants our hearts, not just our actions.

Lent is a time to turn away from bad habits and start fresh with Jesus. No matter what mistakes we've made, God is always ready to forgive us and give us a new beginning.

🚀 **Think About It:**

🟦 What is something in your heart that you need to change?

🟦 How can you grow closer to Jesus during Lent?

🔴 **Challenge**: A Fresh Start List

Write down one thing you want to stop doing and one thing you want to start doing to become more like Jesus.

🙏 **Prayer: A New Heart for Jesus**

Dear Jesus,

As I begin this Lent journey, I want to come closer to You. Help me to let go of things that keep me away from You. Teach me to trust You more every day. Thank You for Your love and mercy. Amen.

Thursday (March 6, 2025)

Day 2: Jesus in the Wilderness

📖 **Bible Reading: Matthew 4:1-11**

"Jesus was led by the Spirit into the wilderness to be tempted by the devil."

💡 **Reflection: Jesus Shows Us How to Be Strong**

Jesus spent 40 days in the wilderness praying and fasting before beginning His mission. While He was there, Satan tried to trick Him into making bad choices, but Jesus stayed strong by using God's Word to fight back.

Just like Jesus, we all face temptations—things that try to pull us away from God. But when we remember God's promises, we can say "no" to temptation and make the right choices.

🚀 **Think About It:**

🔳 Have you ever been tempted to do something

wrong?

■ What can you say or do when you feel tempted?

● **Challenge**: Memorize One of Jesus' Responses

Pick one of the verses Jesus used in the wilderness and memorize it to help you when you face temptation.

🙏 **Prayer: Strength to Make Good Choices**

Dear Jesus,

Thank You for showing me how to resist temptation. Help me to make good choices and trust You when I feel weak. I know You will always be with me. Amen.

Friday (March 7, 2025)

Day 3: The Power of Prayer

📖 **Bible Reading: Matthew 6:6**
"When you pray, go into your room, close the door and pray to your Father, who is unseen."

💡 **Reflection: Talking to God Anytime, Anywhere**

Prayer is simply talking to God. Jesus taught that we don't have to use fancy words or pray just to impress others—God cares about what's in our hearts.

We can pray when we're happy, sad, confused, or thankful. No matter what, God is always listening.

🖋 **Think About It:**
🔲 How often do you talk to God?
🔲 What are some things you can pray about?

● **Challenge**: Create a Prayer Spot

Find a quiet place where you can pray and spend time with God every day.

🙏 **Prayer: Help Me Pray Every Day**

Dear God,

I want to talk to You more. Help me to pray every day and to trust that You always hear me. Thank You for loving me. Amen.

Saturday (March 8, 2025)

Day 4: Why Do We Fast?

📖 **Bible Reading: Matthew 6:16-18**

"When you fast, do not look somber like the hypocrites... but when you fast, anoint your head and wash your face."

💡 **Reflection: Giving Up Something to Grow Closer to God**

Fasting means giving up something for a short time to focus on God. It helps us remember that God is more important than anything else.

People fast from food, video games, or social media—not to punish themselves, but to spend more time with Jesus.

🚀 **Think About It:**

⬛ What is something that distracts you from God?

⬛ How can you use this time to grow closer to Jesus?

● **Challenge**: Try a Mini Fast!

Pick one thing to give up for one day and use that time to pray, read the Bible, or help others.

🙏 **Prayer: Help Me Put You First**

Dear God,

Help me to remember that nothing is more important than You. Teach me to focus on You and to let go of distractions. Amen.

Sunday (March 9, 2025)

Day 5: Giving and Helping Others

📖 **Bible Reading: Luke 6:38**

"Give, and it will be given to you."

🕯 **Reflection: The Joy of Giving**

Have you ever done something kind for someone and felt happy afterward? That's because giving isn't just about helping others—it also fills our own hearts with joy! Jesus teaches that when we give, we receive even more in return—not always in money or gifts, but in love, kindness, and the blessings of God. Giving is a way to show God's love to others, and it reminds us that everything we have is a gift from Him.

Giving doesn't always mean giving money. It can be as simple as sharing your time, helping someone with a small task, or offering a kind word when someone is feeling down. The best kind of giving is the kind that expects nothing in

15

return. When we give with a joyful heart, God sees our kindness and blesses us in ways we may not even expect.

🚀 Think About It:

■ When was the last time you gave something to help someone?

■ How can you show kindness and generosity today?

● Challenge: A Secret Act of Kindness!

Do one act of kindness today without telling anyone!

🕯 Prayer: Help Me Have a Giving Heart

Dear Jesus,

Thank You for blessing me so much! Help me to have a giving heart like Yours and to look for ways to help others every day. Show me how to love and serve people, even when no one is watching. Let my actions bring joy to those around me and glorify You. Amen.

Monday (March 10, 2025)

Day 6: Forgiving Like Jesus

📖 **Bible Reading: Matthew 18:21-22**

"Lord, how many times shall I forgive my brother? ... Jesus answered, 'Not seven times, but seventy-seven times.'"

💡 **Reflection: Forgiving Again and Again**

Forgiving someone who has hurt us is not always easy, but it is what Jesus asks us to do. He tells us to forgive again and again, just like He forgives us. When we hold onto anger, it makes our hearts heavy and fills us with sadness. But when we choose to forgive, we feel peace, and our hearts become lighter. Jesus knows that forgiveness isn't just for the other person—it's for us too! It helps us let go of hurt and move forward with love.

Forgiving doesn't mean forgetting or saying that what happened was okay. It means choosing to let go of anger and not letting it control our hearts. Sometimes, we may need to forgive someone even if they never say sorry. Jesus forgave the people who hurt Him, and He calls us to do the same. When we forgive, we show the world what God's love really looks like.

🚀 Think About It:
■ Is there someone you need to forgive today?

⬤ Challenge: Pray for Someone Who Hurt You
Ask God to bless them and help you let go of any anger.

🙏 Prayer: Help Me Forgive Like You

Dear Jesus,
Thank You for always forgiving me. Help me to forgive others the way You do, even when it's hard. Teach me to love and be kind, even when I feel hurt. Fill my heart with peace, and let me reflect Your love to everyone around me. Amen.

Tuesday (March 11, 2025)

Day 7: Sunday Reflection – Walking with Jesus

📖 **Bible Reading: Proverbs 3:5-6**
"Trust in the Lord with all your heart and lean not on your own understanding."

💡 **Reflection: God's Plan is Always Good**

Sometimes life can be confusing, and we don't always understand why things happen the way they do. Maybe you've prayed for something and it didn't happen the way you expected, or maybe you've faced a difficult situation that made you feel lost. In those moments, Jesus invites us to trust Him completely. Even when we can't see the full picture, God knows exactly what's best for us. He promises that if we follow Him, He will lead us in the right direction.

Walking with Jesus means letting go of our worries and believing that He is in control. It doesn't mean life will always be easy, but it does mean that we are never alone. When we trust Jesus, we can face any challenge knowing that He is guiding us, loving us, and working everything out for our good.

🚀 Think About It:

■ What's one thing you need to trust Jesus with this week?

● Challenge: Let Go and Trust

Write down a worry and give it to Jesus in prayer.

🙏 Prayer: Trusting You Completely

Dear God,
Help me to trust You in everything. Even when I don't understand, I know Your plan is good. Teach me to walk in faith and not in fear. Remind me that You are always with me, guiding me every step of the way. Amen.

Week 2: Learning to Follow Jesus

Monday (March 12, 2025)

Day 8: Jesus Calls His Friends

📖 **Bible Reading: Matthew 4:18-22**

"Come, follow me," Jesus said, "and I will send you out to fish for people." At once they left their nets and followed Him."

💡 **Reflection: Jesus Chooses Ordinary People**

Have you ever been chosen for a special team or project? It feels exciting to be picked! Jesus chose twelve disciples to follow Him—not because they were the smartest, richest, or most powerful, but because they had open hearts and were willing to learn.

Peter, Andrew, James, and John were fishermen, but when Jesus said, "Follow Me," they left everything behind to follow Him. They didn't hesitate or make excuses—they trusted Jesus completely!

Jesus is still calling people today! He wants you to follow Him, too—not just on Sundays, but every day in how you live, love, and trust Him.

✈ Think About It:
◼ What does it mean to follow Jesus?

◼ Is there something in your life you need to leave behind to follow Him more closely?

● Challenge: Say "Yes" to Jesus Today
Think of one way you can follow Jesus more closely today—maybe by showing kindness, helping someone, or reading your Bible.

⚭ Prayer: A Willing Heart

Dear Jesus,
Thank You for calling me to follow You. Help me to trust You like the disciples did and to say "yes" to You every day. I want to be Your friend and live the way You teach. Amen.

Tuesday (March 13, 2025)

Day 9: The Beatitudes – A Happy Heart

📖 **Bible Reading: Matthew 5:1-12**
"Blessed are the pure in heart, for they will see God."

📍 **Reflection: What It Really Means to Be Blessed**

When we hear the word "blessed," we might think of having lots of money, getting good grades, or receiving gifts. But Jesus teaches us that true blessings come from the heart, not from things. In the Beatitudes, Jesus tells us that those who are humble, kind, merciful, and pure in heart are the ones who are truly blessed. Even when life is hard or we face challenges, we can still find joy and peace when we live the way Jesus teaches.

Following the Beatitudes means choosing to love others, show kindness, and put God first. When we are gentle instead of angry, when we help others instead of only thinking about ourselves, and when we trust God even in difficult times, we receive the kind of happiness that doesn't fade. The world may not always see these as blessings, but God does! True happiness comes not from what we have, but from how we love, serve, and trust Jesus.

🚀 Think About It:
◼ What does it mean to have a happy heart?
◼ How can you live out one of the Beatitudes this week?

● Challenge: Practice a Beatitude Today
Choose one Beatitude (like being merciful or a peacemaker) and live it out today.

🙏 Prayer: A Heart Like Jesus'

Dear Jesus,
Help me to have a heart like Yours—kind, humble, and full of love. Teach me that true

happiness comes from following You, not from things. Show me how to live out the Beatitudes every day and to be a blessing to those around me. Let my heart always seek You first. Amen.

Day 10: The Greatest Commandment

📖 **Bible Reading: Matthew 22:36-40**

*"Love the Lord your God with all your heart...
and love your neighbor as yourself."*

💡 **Reflection: Love is the Most Important
Thing**

Love is the greatest gift we can give and receive.
Jesus tells us that the most important thing we
can do is love God with all our hearts and love
others as ourselves. This means putting God
first in everything—trusting Him, talking to Him,
and obeying His Word. Loving others means
being kind, forgiving, patient, and helpful, even
when it's hard. Love is not just about words; it's
about how we treat people every day.

When we love like Jesus, we bring light into the
world. Imagine a world where everyone followed

this command—where people helped each other, forgave quickly, and treated everyone with kindness. That's the kind of love Jesus wants us to share! When we choose love, we reflect God's heart and show others what it means to be His children.

🚀 Think About It:

🔲 How can you show love to God this week?

🔲 Who in your life needs to feel God's love through you?

⬤ Challenge: Show Love in a Big Way

Do something special today to show love—write a kind note, help a friend, or say "thank you" to someone who helps you.

🙏 Prayer: Teach Me to Love

Dear God,
Help me to love You with my whole heart and to show kindness to others. Let my words and actions spread Your love everywhere I go. Show me how to love even when it's difficult, and help

me to be a light in the lives of those around me. Amen.

Day 11: Jesus Feeds the Hungry

📖 **Bible Reading: John 6:1-14**
"Then Jesus took the loaves, gave thanks, and distributed to those who were seated as much as they wanted."

💡 **Reflection: A Small Gift Can Make a Big Difference**

A little boy had only five loaves of bread and two fish, but he gave them to Jesus. With that small gift, Jesus performed a miracle and fed over 5,000 people! This story reminds us that even the smallest gifts, when given to God, can make a big difference. No matter how little we have, when we share with others, God multiplies it and blesses it in ways we could never imagine.

Sometimes we might feel like we don't have much to give, but generosity isn't just about money—it's about time, kindness, and love. A kind word, a helping hand, or a simple prayer for someone can make a huge impact. Jesus teaches us that when we share, we reflect His love and help bring joy to others.

🚀 Think About It:

■ What do you have that you can share with someone in need?

● Challenge: Give Like Jesus

Find a way to give today—share a snack, donate something, or help a friend.

🙏 Prayer: A Giving Heart

Dear Jesus,

Thank You for providing everything I need. Help me to be generous and to trust that You can do big things with small gifts. Show me how to give with a joyful heart, and use my kindness to bless others. Let my actions bring glory to You. Amen.

Friday (March 16, 2025)

Day 12: Jesus Calms the Storm

📖 **Bible Reading: Mark 4:35-41**
"Quiet! Be still!" Then the wind died down, and it was completely calm."

💡 **Reflection: Trusting Jesus in the Storms of Life**

Life can feel like a storm sometimes—unexpected things happen, we feel worried, or we don't know what to do. The disciples felt the same way when they were caught in a dangerous storm at sea. But when Jesus spoke to the storm, it immediately stopped. This miracle shows us that Jesus has the power to bring peace, no matter how big the storm.

Jesus is always with us, even when life feels scary. He asks us to trust Him and not be afraid. When we put our faith in Jesus, He calms the storms in our hearts and gives us peace, strength, and hope.

🚀 Think About It:

◾ What "storm" are you facing right now?

● Challenge: Write a "Trust Letter" to Jesus

Write a short letter telling Jesus what's worrying you, then pray and trust Him.

🙏 Prayer: Help Me Trust You

Dear Jesus,

Sometimes life feels stormy and scary. Help me to trust that You are always with me and can bring peace to my heart. No matter what I face, remind me that You are bigger than any problem. I put my trust in You today and always. Amen.

Day 13: Jesus Heals the Sick

📖 **Bible Reading: Mark 2:1-12**

"Son, your sins are forgiven... Get up, take your mat, and walk."

💡 **Reflection: Jesus Has the Power to Heal**

One day, a group of friends brought a paralyzed man to Jesus, hoping He would heal him. The house was so crowded that they couldn't get inside, so they climbed up on the roof and lowered their friend down to Jesus! Because of their faith, Jesus not only healed the man physically but also forgave his sins. This story reminds us that Jesus cares about both our bodies and our hearts.

Jesus still heals today—sometimes in big, miraculous ways and sometimes in quiet ways through doctors, medicine, or even the comfort we feel when we pray. Whether we are sick, sad, or hurting inside, we can always turn to Jesus for healing and strength. He sees our pain and walks with us through every difficult moment.

✈ Think About It:

◼ Do you know someone who needs healing?

◼ How can you be a good friend to someone who is hurting?

● **Challenge**: Pray for Someone Who's Sick
Take time today to pray for healing for someone in need. If possible, do something kind for them—send a note, make a call, or just offer encouragement.

⚔ Prayer: Healing and Strength

Dear Jesus,
Thank You for Your power to heal. Please help those who are sick or hurting, and give me faith to trust You always. Help me to be a friend who brings hope and love to those in need. Remind me that no matter what, You are with us, bringing peace and strength. Amen.

Day 14: Trusting Jesus in Hard Times

📖 **Bible Reading: Proverbs 3:5-6**

"Trust in the Lord with all your heart and lean not on your own understanding."

💡 **Reflection: God's Plan is Always Good**

Sometimes, we don't understand why things happen. We might feel confused, disappointed, or even afraid. But Jesus wants us to trust Him, even when we don't have all the answers. God's plan is always good, and He sees the whole picture, even when we don't.

Walking with Jesus means letting go of worry and believing that He is in control. When we put our trust in Him, we can find peace, hope, and strength no matter what happens.

🚀 Think About It:

🔲 What's one thing you need to trust Jesus with this week?

🔴 Challenge: Let Go and Trust

Write down a worry and give it to Jesus in prayer.

🙏 Prayer: Trusting You Completely

Dear God,

Help me to trust You in everything. Even when I don't understand, I know Your plan is good. Teach me to have faith in You and to follow You with my whole heart. Thank You for always being with me. Amen.

Week 3: Loving Others Like Jesus

Day 15: The Parable of the Lost Sheep

📖 **Bible Reading: Luke 15:3-7**

"Rejoice with me; I have found my lost sheep."

💡 **Reflection: God Never Gives Up on Us**

Have you ever lost something really important to you, like a favorite toy or a special gift? You probably searched everywhere until you found it. That's exactly how Jesus describes God's love in the Parable of the Lost Sheep. He tells a story of a shepherd who had 100 sheep but lost just one. Instead of saying, "I still have 99," the shepherd left everything to find the missing one. When he finally found it, he was so happy that he celebrated!

This story reminds us that every single person matters to God. Sometimes, we may feel far from Him or think we've messed up too much. But

God never stops looking for us. He loves us so much that He rejoices when we come back to Him. No matter how lost we feel, we are never too far from God's love.

🚀 **Think About It:**
◼ Have you ever felt lost or far from God?
◼ How does it feel to know that God never stops searching for you?

⬤ **Challenge**: Be a Shepherd of Kindness
Reach out to someone who may feel lonely or left out. Show them they are loved!

🙏 **Prayer: Help Me to See Your Love**

Dear Jesus,
Thank You for never giving up on me. When I feel lost, remind me that You are always looking for me with love. Help me to care for others like You care for me. Let my heart be full of kindness and love. Amen.

Thursday (March 20, 2025)

📌 Day 16: Jesus Welcomes Children

📖 **Bible Reading: Mark 10:13-16**

"Let the little children come to me, and do not hinder them, for the kingdom of God belongs to such as these."

💡 **Reflection: You Are Special to Jesus**

Sometimes, people think that only grown-ups matter in church or that kids don't understand faith as much. But Jesus showed that children are just as important as anyone else! In this story, people tried to stop children from coming to Jesus, but He welcomed them with open arms. He even said that we should all have faith like children—trusting, loving, and believing in Him with all our hearts.

Jesus wants you to know that you are important to Him. He loves the way you laugh, learn, and care for others. He listens when you pray, and He delights in your faith. You don't have to wait until you're older to follow Jesus—you can love Him and share His kindness right now!

🚀 **Think About It:**

⬛ What do you think it means to have childlike faith?

⬛ How can you show love for Jesus today?

⬤ **Challenge:** Show Jesus' Love to Another Kid

Be kind to someone today—include them in a game, give a smile, or pray for them.

🔥 **Prayer: Help Me Trust You Like a Child**

Dear Jesus,

Thank You for loving me just as I am. Help me to trust You with all my heart and to love You like a child—fully and joyfully. Teach me to share Your love with everyone around me. Amen.

Friday (March 21, 2025)

Day 17: The Good Samaritan

📖 **Bible Reading: Luke 10:25-37**
"Love your neighbor as yourself."

💡 **Reflection: Loving Everyone, Even When It's Hard**

Imagine walking down the street and seeing someone hurt, but no one stops to help. That's what happened in the story of the Good Samaritan. A man was attacked and left injured, and many people walked past him, not wanting to get involved. But one man—a Samaritan—stopped, helped him, and took care of him, even though they were from different backgrounds.

Jesus told this story to show us that loving others means helping everyone, not just our friends or people like us. Real love isn't about choosing who deserves kindness—it's about being kind no matter what. Jesus calls us to be like the

Good Samaritan, always ready to show compassion and care.

🚀 Think About It:

⬛ Who is someone in your life that needs kindness?

⬛ How can you be a "Good Samaritan" today?

● **Challenge**: Find a Way to Help Someone Today

Look for someone who needs help and do something kind for them.

🙏 Prayer: Help Me Love Like You

Dear Jesus,

Teach me to love everyone, not just my friends. Help me to be kind, even when it's hard. Give me a heart like Yours, full of compassion and care for others. Amen.

Saturday (March 22, 2025)

Day 18: The Prodigal Son – A Loving Father

📖 **Bible Reading: Luke 15:11-32**

"But while he was still a long way off, his father saw him and was filled with compassion for him."

💡 **Reflection: God's Love Never Runs Out**

Have you ever made a mistake and felt too embarrassed to say sorry? That's what happened in this story. The Prodigal Son left home, wasted everything he had, and thought his father would never take him back. But when he returned, instead of being angry, his father ran to him, hugged him, and welcomed him home with joy.

This story shows us that God's love never runs out. Even when we make mistakes, He is always waiting with open arms. No matter how far we feel from Him, He never stops loving us. We can always return to God, and He will forgive, restore, and celebrate us!

🚀 Think About It:

■ Have you ever felt like you let someone down?

■ How does it feel to know that God always welcomes you back?

⬤ Challenge: Say Sorry and Make Things Right

If you've hurt someone, apologize and try to fix the situation.

🙏 Prayer: Thank You for Your Forgiveness

Dear Jesus,

Thank You for always welcoming me back, no matter what. When I make mistakes, remind me that Your love never ends. Help me to show forgiveness and love to others like You do. Amen.

Day 19: The Widow's Offering – Giving with Love

📖 **Bible Reading: Mark 12:41-44**

"She put in everything—all she had to live on."

💡 **Reflection: Giving from the Heart**

Jesus saw a poor widow give two small coins in the offering, while others gave lots of money. Even though she gave very little, Jesus said her gift was the greatest because she gave with love and trust in God. She didn't give because she had to—she gave because she loved God.

This story teaches us that it's not about how much we give, but how we give. Whether it's money, time, or kindness, Jesus wants us to give from the heart. Even small acts of generosity can make a big difference when done with love.

🚀 Think About It:

◼ What's something small you can give that could make a big impact?

⬤ Challenge: Give Something from Your Heart

Share your time, talents, or kindness with someone today.

🙏 Prayer: A Giving Heart Like Yours

Dear Jesus,

Help me to give with love, not just out of duty. Show me ways to share kindness, time, and blessings with others. Let my heart always be generous, just like Yours. Amen.

Day 20: Jesus and Zacchaeus – A Changed Heart

📖 **Bible Reading: Luke 19:1-10**

"For the Son of Man came to seek and to save the lost."

💡 **Reflection: Jesus Changes Hearts**

Zacchaeus was a rich tax collector, but he wasn't well-liked because he took extra money from people. One day, he heard that Jesus was coming to town, and he was so eager to see Him that he climbed a tree just to get a better view! Even though many people didn't like Zacchaeus, Jesus saw him, called him by name, and even chose to visit his house. That one encounter changed Zacchaeus' heart—he repented, gave back the money he had taken, and chose to live a new life.

This story shows that Jesus sees past our mistakes and loves us anyway. No matter who we are or what we have done, He is always ready to welcome us and help us change for the better. When we truly meet Jesus, our hearts become kinder, more honest, and more loving. Just like Zacchaeus, we can choose to live differently and share God's love with others.

🚀 Think About It:

■ How do you think Zacchaeus felt when Jesus called him by name?

■ What's one way you can change to be more like Jesus?

⬤ Challenge: Make Things Right

If you've wronged someone, apologize and try to make it right, just like Zacchaeus did.

🔥 Prayer: A Heart That Follows You

Dear Jesus,

Thank You for loving me even when I make mistakes. Help me to have a heart like Zacchaeus—one that wants to change and do what is right. Show me how to live in a way that pleases You and blesses others. Let my actions reflect Your love every day. Amen.

Day 21: How Can I Show God's Love?

📖 **Bible Reading: 1 John 4:7**

"Dear friends, let us love one another, for love comes from God."

💡 **Reflection: Living Out God's Love**

God's love is not just something we receive—it's something we are called to share. Jesus teaches us that love isn't just about saying kind words, but about showing kindness through our actions. When we help a friend, forgive someone who hurt us, share with those in need, or even pray for others, we are living out God's love.

Sometimes, loving others can be difficult, especially when people are unkind or when we don't feel like it. But love is a choice—one that Jesus made every day, even when it was hard. When we love like Jesus, we bring light and joy into the world. No act of love is ever too small; even a smile or a kind word can change someone's day.

🚀 **Think About It:**
🟦 How have you shown God's love this week?
🟦 What's one new way you can love like Jesus?

🔴 **Challenge:** Show Love in Action
Find one way today to show God's love—write an encouraging note, help a family member, or simply be a good friend.

🙏 **Prayer: Help Me Love Like You**

Dear Jesus,
Teach me to love the way You do—with patience, kindness, and a joyful heart. Help me to see opportunities every day to share Your love with others. Let my actions, words, and choices reflect Your light in the world. Thank You for loving me first so I can love others. Amen

Week 4: Walking with Jesus Toward the Cross

Day 22: Jesus Enters Jerusalem (Palm Sunday)

📖 **Bible Reading: Matthew 21:1-11**

"Hosanna to the Son of David! Blessed is he who comes in the name of the Lord!"

💡 **Reflection: Welcoming Jesus with Joy**

Imagine a big parade where everyone is cheering, waving flags, and celebrating. That's what happened when Jesus entered Jerusalem riding on a donkey. The people were so excited that they laid down their cloaks and palm branches, shouting, "Hosanna!", which means "Save us!" They welcomed Jesus as their King, but they didn't fully understand what kind of King He was.

Jesus didn't come to be a rich and powerful ruler—He came to save us through love and sacrifice. Even though the same people who cheered for Him would later turn against Him, He still chose to follow God's plan. Just like the crowd welcomed Jesus into Jerusalem, we should welcome Him into our hearts every day!

🚀 Think About It:
■ How can you celebrate Jesus in your life?
■ Have you truly welcomed Jesus into your heart?

● Challenge: Wave Your "Palm Branch" for Jesus
Write down a praise or thank-you prayer to Jesus today.

🙏 Prayer: A Heart That Welcomes You

Dear Jesus,
Thank You for coming to save us. Help me to always welcome You into my heart with joy. Teach me to celebrate Your love and to follow You with all my heart. Let my life bring You praise every day. Amen.

Thursday (March 27, 2025)

Day 23: Jesus Washes His Disciples' Feet

📖 **Bible Reading: John 13:1-17**

"Now that I, your Lord and Teacher, have washed your feet, you also should wash one another's feet."

💡 **Reflection: Serving Others Like Jesus**

Have you ever done a chore that you didn't really want to do? Maybe washing dishes, taking out the trash, or cleaning your room? Jesus, the Son of God, did something even more surprising—He washed His disciples' feet! In Jesus' time, people walked on dusty roads in sandals, and washing feet was the job of a servant. But Jesus, their teacher and Lord, got down on His knees to serve them.

Jesus did this to teach us that true greatness comes from serving others. He wants us to be humble and help people, even when it's not easy. When we choose kindness, help without being asked, and put others first, we are following Jesus' example of love and humility.

🚀 **Think About It:**

⬛ What is one way you can serve others today?

⬛ How can you be humble like Jesus?

🔴 **Challenge**: Serve Like Jesus

Do something kind for someone without being asked—help a sibling, clean up, or write an encouraging note.

🕯 **Prayer: A Servant's Heart**

Dear Jesus,

Thank You for showing me how to love by serving others. Help me to be humble, kind, and willing to help, even in small ways. Let my actions reflect Your love to everyone around me. Amen.

Friday (March 28, 2025)

Day 24: The Last Supper - A Special Meal

📖 **Bible Reading: Luke 22:14-20**
"Do this in remembrance of me."

💡 **Reflection: Remembering Jesus' Love**

Have you ever had a special family dinner where everyone gathered together? That's what Jesus did at the Last Supper—He shared a special meal with His disciples before going to the cross. But this was more than just dinner—it was a reminder of His love and sacrifice.

During the meal, Jesus took bread and wine and told His disciples that they represented His body and blood, given for us. Today, we still remember this through Communion, where we reflect on Jesus' great love. Every time we eat and drink in His name, we remember that He gave everything for us so we could be with Him forever.

🚀 Think About It:

◼ What does it mean to "remember Jesus"?

◼ How can you show gratitude for His sacrifice?

● Challenge: A Thankful Heart

Write a prayer thanking Jesus for His love and sacrifice.

🙏 Prayer: Remembering Your Love

Dear Jesus,

Thank You for giving Your life for me. Help me to always remember and honor Your love. Teach me to be grateful and to live in a way that shows Your kindness to others. Amen.

Saturday (March 29, 2025)

Day 25: Jesus Prays in the Garden

📖 **Bible Reading: Matthew 26:36-46**
"Yet not as I will, but as You will."

🕯 **Reflection: Trusting God When It's Hard**

Have you ever faced a really tough moment—one where you felt scared, nervous, or didn't know what to do? That's how Jesus felt in the Garden of Gethsemane. He knew He was about to suffer, and He was overwhelmed. But instead of running away, He prayed to His Father, saying, "Not my will, but Yours be done."

Even when things are difficult, Jesus teaches us to trust God's plan. Sometimes, we may not understand why things happen, but we can always pray, trust, and know that God is in control. When we are afraid or struggling, we can talk to God just like Jesus did.

✒ Think About It:

■ What is something you need to trust God with?

■ How can prayer help you when you feel afraid?

● Challenge: Pray Like Jesus

Take a few minutes today to talk to God about your worries and trust Him.

🙏 Prayer: Trusting You in Everything

Dear Jesus,

When life is hard, help me to trust You just like You trusted the Father. Give me the courage to follow Your plan and to believe that You are always with me. Thank You for hearing my prayers and giving me peace. Amen.

Sunday (March 30, 2025)

📌 Day 26: Jesus is Betrayed

📖 Bible Reading: Luke 22:47-53

"Judas, are you betraying the Son of Man with a kiss?"

💡 Reflection: Staying Faithful to Jesus

Have you ever had a friend let you down or break a promise? That's what happened to Jesus when Judas, one of His own disciples, betrayed Him. Judas had followed Jesus, listened to His teachings, and even saw His miracles, but in the end, he chose money over loyalty. He betrayed Jesus with a kiss, a sign that was supposed to mean friendship.

Even though Jesus knew Judas would betray Him, He still loved and forgave him. This reminds us that even when people hurt us, we should choose forgiveness instead of anger. It also teaches us to stay faithful to Jesus no matter what. Following Jesus means choosing His way over the world's way, even when it's hard.

🚀 Think About It:

🔲 Why is it important to stay faithful to Jesus?

🔲 How can you show loyalty to God this week?

● Challenge: Choose Jesus Over Everything

Make a commitment to follow Jesus' way even when it's hard.

🙏 Prayer: A Faithful Heart

Dear Jesus,

Even when others turn away, help me to stay faithful to You. Give me a heart that chooses love, forgiveness, and truth, even when it's difficult. Help me to always put You first. Amen.

Monday (March 31, 2025)

Day 27: Jesus on Trial

📖 **Bible Reading: Matthew 27:11-26**
"What shall I do, then, with Jesus who is called the Messiah?" Pilate asked. They all answered, 'Crucify Him!'"

💡 **Reflection: Standing for What is Right**

Have you ever been blamed for something you didn't do? It feels unfair, right? That's what happened to Jesus when He was put on trial. Even though He was innocent, people lied about Him, and the leaders wanted Him punished. Pilate, the governor, knew Jesus had done nothing wrong, but he was afraid of the crowd. Instead of standing up for what was right, he let the people decide—and they chose to crucify Jesus.

Even when everything was unfair, Jesus didn't fight back or get angry. He trusted that God's plan was greater. Sometimes, we might face situations where people don't treat us fairly. But just like Jesus, we can choose to trust God, be kind, and do what is right, even when it's hard. Jesus showed us that true strength comes from trusting God and following His ways.

🚀 Think About It:

⬛ Have you ever been treated unfairly? How did you react?

⬛ How can you trust God when things don't seem fair?

⚫ Challenge: Do What is Right

No matter what happens today, choose to be honest, kind, and fair—even if others are not.

🙏 Prayer: Strength to Trust You

Dear Jesus,

Even when life is unfair, help me to stand for what is right. Teach me to trust You, even when things don't go my way. Give me the strength to follow You no matter what happens. Amen.

Day 28:   Trusting God's Plan

📖 Bible Reading: Romans 8:28

"And we know that in all things God works for the good of those who love Him, who have been called according to His purpose."

💡 Reflection: God's Plan is Always Good

Sometimes, life doesn't go the way we expect. We might face challenges, disappointments, or things that feel confusing. When Jesus was arrested, put on trial, and sentenced to die, His disciples probably felt scared and hopeless. But even though things seemed bad, God was working through it all to bring salvation to the world.

Just like Jesus trusted God's plan, we can trust God even when life feels hard. God's plan is bigger than anything we can see right now, and He always brings good from even the most difficult situations. When we feel uncertain or afraid, we can remember that God is in control, and His love never fails.

✈ Think About It:

🔲 Is there something in your life that is hard to understand right now?

🔲 How can you trust God even when things seem uncertain?

● Challenge: Let Go and Trust

Write down something you are worried about and pray for God's help to trust His plan.

🙏 Prayer: Trusting You Completely

Dear Jesus,

Sometimes, I don't understand why things happen, but I know You are always with me. Help me to trust Your plan, even when I can't see the whole picture. Remind me that Your love never fails and that You are always working for my good. Let my heart rest in Your promises. Amen.

Week 5: God's Love Shown Through Jesus

Day 29: Jesus Carries the Cross

📖 **Bible Reading: John 19:17**

"Carrying his own cross, he went out to the place of the Skull (which in Aramaic is called Golgotha)."

💡 **Reflection: Carrying the Weight for Us**

Have you ever had to carry something really heavy? Maybe a big backpack, a pile of books, or even a load of groceries? It can make you feel tired and worn out. Now, imagine carrying a huge wooden cross after being beaten and hurt. That's what Jesus did for us. Even though He had never done anything wrong, He was given the burden of carrying His cross to the place where He would be crucified.

Jesus didn't deserve to suffer, but He carried the cross out of love for us. He took on our pain and sins so that we could be forgiven. Just like

Jesus carried His cross, sometimes we have struggles in life too. It may be doing what's right when others don't, or standing up for our faith when it's hard. But we don't carry our burdens alone—Jesus walks with us every step of the way.

🚀 Think About It:

🟦 Have you ever had to do something difficult for the right reason?

🟦 How does it feel to know that Jesus carried the cross for you?

🔴 Challenge: Carry Someone's Burden Today

Find a way to help someone who is struggling—it could be a kind word, a prayer, or lending a helping hand.

🙏 Prayer: Strength to Walk with You

Dear Jesus,

Thank You for carrying the cross for me. Even though it was painful, You did it because You love me. Help me to carry my own cross—to do what is right, even when it's hard. Give me strength, and remind me that I am never alone. I trust You to help me every step of the way. Amen.

The Crucifixion (April 3, 2025)

📌 Day 30: – Jesus' Great Love

📖 **Bible Reading: Luke 23:33-46**
"Father, forgive them, for they do not know what they are doing."

🕯 **Reflection: The Greatest Act of Love**

Have you ever been treated unfairly? Maybe someone blamed you for something you didn't do, or a friend hurt your feelings. Now imagine being completely innocent, yet being punished in the worst way possible. That's what happened to Jesus on the cross. He had never sinned, but He chose to take our place so that we could be saved. Even while suffering, He still forgave the people who hurt Him.

The cross is the greatest symbol of love. Jesus could have stopped everything, but He stayed because He loves us. His sacrifice means that no matter what we've done, we can be forgiven.

When we look at the cross, we see God's incredible love for us—a love that never gives up.

🚀 Think About It:

■ How does it make you feel to know that Jesus willingly died for you?

■ What can you do to show love and forgiveness like Jesus did?

⬤ Challenge: Show Forgiveness Today

If someone has hurt you, choose to forgive them, just as Jesus forgave.

🙏 Prayer: Thank You for the Cross

Dear Jesus,

Thank You for loving me so much that You gave Your life for me. Help me to never forget the sacrifice You made. Teach me to love and forgive others, just like You did on the cross. Let me always remember that Your love is bigger than my mistakes. Amen.

Friday (April 4, 2025)

Day 31: Jesus' Last Words on the Cross

📖 **Bible Reading: John 19:30**
"It is finished."

💡 **Reflection: Jesus Completed His Mission**

Have you ever worked hard on something and finally finished it? Maybe it was a big school project, a puzzle, or a race. There's a feeling of accomplishment when something important is completed. On the cross, Jesus' last words were, "It is finished." But He wasn't just talking about His life—He had completed His mission to save us.

When Jesus said, "It is finished," He meant that our sins were paid for and that His love had made a way for us to be with God forever. We don't have to earn God's love or forgiveness—Jesus already did the work for us.

All we have to do is accept His gift and follow Him.

🚀 Think About It:

■ What do you think Jesus meant by "It is finished"?

■ How can you live knowing that Jesus has already won the victory for you?

● Challenge: Thank Jesus for His Gift

Take a moment today to pray and thank Jesus for what He finished on the cross.

🙏 Prayer: Grateful for Your Victory

Dear Jesus,

Thank You for completing Your mission to save us. Because of You, I am free and forgiven. Help me to live in Your love every day and to share Your victory with others. Let my heart always be filled with gratitude. Amen.

Saturday (April 5, 2025)

Day 32: Jesus is Buried

📖 **Bible Reading: Matthew 27:57-61**

"Joseph took the body, wrapped it in a clean linen cloth, and placed it in his own new tomb."

🕯 **Reflection: A Time of Silence and Waiting**

After Jesus died on the cross, His body was placed in a tomb. The world must have felt so quiet and sad. The disciples were heartbroken, and it seemed like all hope was gone. But God was still working behind the scenes. Even when it looked like the end, something amazing was about to happen.

Sometimes, we feel like we are in a time of waiting—praying for something, hoping for answers, or feeling unsure about the future. But just like that silent Saturday, God is always working, even when we don't see it. We can trust that He is in control and has a plan for everything.

🚀 Think About It:

◼ Have you ever felt like you were waiting for something and didn't know what would happen?

◼ How can you trust God in moments when things feel silent?

● Challenge: Trust in God's Timing

Write down something you are waiting for and pray for patience and trust.

🙏 Prayer: Trusting You in the Waiting

Dear Jesus,

Even when I don't see what You are doing, help me to trust that You are always at work. Give me patience and faith to believe that Your plan is always good. Thank You for always being near, even in the quiet moments. Amen.

Day 33: Waiting in Hope

📖 **Bible Reading: John 16:22**

"Now is your time of grief, but I will see you again, and you will rejoice, and no one will take away your joy."

💡 **Reflection: Trusting God in the Silence**

Have you ever waited for something really important? Maybe a special trip, a birthday, or a big surprise? The waiting can feel long, but when the moment finally comes, it's worth it. On Holy Saturday, Jesus' followers were waiting too—but instead of excitement, they felt sad and lost. Jesus was in the tomb, and it seemed like all hope was gone.

But even in the silence, God was still at work. The disciples didn't know what was coming, but we do—Easter morning was just around the corner! Holy Saturday reminds us that even when life feels quiet, confusing, or hard, God's plan is still moving forward. We may not see it right away, but hope is never lost when we trust in Jesus.

🖋 Think About It:

🔲 Have you ever felt like you were waiting for an answer from God?

🔲 How can you remind yourself to trust Him, even when you don't see what's happening?

● Challenge: Hold onto Hope

Write a letter to Jesus, telling Him what you're trusting Him with, even if you don't understand everything yet.

🙏 Prayer: Trusting You Even in the Waiting

Dear Jesus,

Sometimes, waiting is hard. When I don't see answers or feel unsure about what's next, help me to trust that You are still working. Thank You for always keeping Your promises. Fill my heart with hope as I wait on You. Amen.

Monday (April 7, 2025)

Day 34: Why Did Jesus Die for Us?

📖 **Bible Reading: Romans 5:8**

"But God demonstrates His own love for us in this: While we were still sinners, Christ died for us."

💡 **Reflection: A Love That Never Fails**

Imagine making a really big mistake—one that you know has serious consequences. Now imagine that someone else steps in and takes the punishment for you, even though they didn't do anything wrong. That's exactly what Jesus did for us. Even though we make mistakes and sin, Jesus chose to take our place on the cross.

He didn't wait for us to be perfect—He loved us even when we were lost. That's how big His love is! Jesus' death wasn't just a sad moment—it was a powerful act of love that opened the way for us to be close to God forever. Because of Jesus, we are forgiven, we are loved, and we are never alone.

🚀 Think About It:

■ How does it make you feel to know that Jesus died for you, even before you knew Him?

■ How can you show gratitude for His sacrifice?

● Challenge: Share the Good News

Tell one person today about Jesus' love and what He did for them.

🙏 Prayer: Thank You for Your Amazing Love

Dear Jesus,

I don't deserve Your love, but You gave it to me anyway. Thank You for dying for me and taking my place. Help me to always remember Your sacrifice and to live in a way that honors You. Fill my heart with Your love so that I can share it with others. Amen.

Day 35: What Jesus Did for Me

📖 **Bible Reading: 2 Corinthians 5:17**

"Therefore, if anyone is in Christ, the new creation has come: The old has gone, the new is here!"

💡 **Reflection: A Brand New Life**

Have you ever gotten a fresh start? Maybe a new school year, a clean room, or a second chance after a mistake? When Jesus died for us, He gave us the ultimate fresh start. Because of His sacrifice, we are no longer stuck in our sins—we are made new in Him!

Jesus didn't just save us from something—He saved us for something. He gave us new life so that we can live for Him, love others, and share His goodness. Every day, we have the chance to walk in freedom, joy, and purpose because of what Jesus did for us. Our old life is gone, and our new life in Him has begun!

🚀 Think About It:

🟥 What does it mean to be made new in Jesus?

🟥 How can you live differently because of what Jesus has done?

🔴 Challenge: Live Like a New Creation

Think of one way you can live for Jesus this week—whether in kindness, forgiveness, or sharing His love.

🙏 Prayer: Thank You for Making Me New

Dear Jesus,

Because of You, I am a new creation. My past mistakes don't define me anymore—You do. Thank You for giving me a fresh start every day. Help me to live in a way that shows Your love to the world. I want to follow You with all my heart. Amen.

Week 6: Jesus is Alive!

Day 36: The Empty Tomb (Resurrection Sunday!)

📖 **Bible Reading: Matthew 28:1-10**

"He is not here; He has risen, just as He said!"

💡 **Reflection: Jesus is Alive!**

Imagine waking up on Easter morning, expecting everything to be normal, but then finding out the greatest news ever—Jesus is alive! That's exactly what happened to the women who went to Jesus' tomb. They thought they were going to find His body, but instead, they found an empty tomb and an angel who told them that Jesus had risen!

Easter isn't just about candy and eggs—it's about celebrating the greatest victory in history! Jesus defeated sin and death so that we can have new life with Him. Because He is alive, we don't have to be afraid of anything. We can have hope, joy, and a forever friendship with Him!

🚀 Think About It:
■ How do you feel knowing that Jesus is alive?
■ What does Easter mean to you?

● Challenge: Spread the Easter Joy!
Tell one person today about the true meaning of Easter.

🙏 Prayer: Thank You for New Life

Dear Jesus,
Thank You for defeating death and rising again! Because You live, I can have hope and joy every day. Help me to celebrate Your love and share it with others. I am so thankful for You! Amen.

Thursday (April 10, 2025)

Day 37: Jesus Appears to His Friends

📖 **Bible Reading: Luke 24:36-49**
"Peace be with you."

💡 **Reflection: Jesus Brings Peace**

Have you ever been scared or confused about something? That's exactly how Jesus' friends felt after He died. They had lost hope, and they didn't know what to do. But then, Jesus appeared to them! Even though the doors were locked, He suddenly stood among them and said, "Peace be with you."

Jesus brings peace, comfort, and joy to our hearts, just like He did for His disciples. No matter what we are facing, we can trust that Jesus is always with us. We don't have to be afraid because He is alive and He loves us!

Think About It:

■ When have you felt scared and needed Jesus' peace?

■ How can you remember that Jesus is always with you?

Challenge: Spread Jesus' Peace

Do something today to bring peace—help a friend, be kind, or pray for someone in need.

Prayer: Fill My Heart with Your Peace

Dear Jesus,

Just like You calmed Your friends' fears, calm my heart when I feel afraid. Help me to trust that You are always with me. Fill me with Your peace and help me to share it with others. Amen.

Friday (April 11, 2025)

Day 38: Doubting Thomas Learns to Believe

📖 **Bible Reading: John 20:24-29**
"Blessed are those who have not seen and yet have believed."

🔦 **Reflection: Trusting in Jesus Even When We Can't See Him**

Have you ever had trouble believing something until you saw it with your own eyes? That's what happened to Thomas, one of Jesus' disciples. When the others told him that Jesus was alive, he didn't believe them. He said, "I won't believe it until I see Jesus and touch His scars." A week later, Jesus appeared and showed Thomas His hands and side. Thomas finally believed, but Jesus said, "Blessed are those who believe without seeing."

Sometimes, we might struggle to trust God because we can't see Him. But faith means believing even when we don't have all the answers. Jesus wants us to trust Him, even when we can't see everything clearly.

🚀 **Think About It:**

◼ Have you ever had a hard time believing something?

◼ How can you grow your faith in Jesus every day?

● **Challenge:** Strengthen Your Faith

Take a moment to pray and thank Jesus for being with you, even when you can't see Him.

🙏 **Prayer: Help Me Believe**

Dear Jesus,

Sometimes, I have doubts, just like Thomas. Help me to trust You even when I can't see everything clearly. Grow my faith and remind me that You are always with me. Amen.

Saturday (April 12, 2025)

Day 39: The Great Commission – Go and Tell!

📖 **Bible Reading: Matthew 28:16-20**
"Go and make disciples of all nations."

💡 **Reflection: Sharing the Good News**

Have you ever been so excited about something that you couldn't wait to tell your friends? Maybe it was a new game, a fun trip, or a big surprise. That's how Jesus' disciples felt after He rose from the dead! Jesus gave them an important mission—go and tell the whole world about Him!

Jesus calls us to do the same. We don't have to preach to thousands of people, but we can share His love with our words, actions, and kindness. Whether it's telling a friend about Jesus, helping someone in need, or showing kindness, we can be part of His great mission.

Think About It:

■ How can you tell others about Jesus?

■ What are some ways you can show Jesus' love to others?

● **Challenge**: Be a Messenger for Jesus

Find one way today to share Jesus with someone—a kind word, a prayer, or telling a friend about Him.

Prayer: Help Me Share Your Love

Dear Jesus,

Thank You for trusting me to share Your love with others. Help me to be bold in telling others about You. Show me ways to spread kindness and joy wherever I go. Amen.

Sunday (April 13, 2025)

Day 40: Jesus Goes to Heaven (Ascension Day)

📖 **Bible Reading: Acts 1:6-11**
"You will receive power when the Holy Spirit comes on you; and you will be my witnesses to the ends of the earth."

💡 **Reflection: Jesus is Always with Us**

Imagine saying goodbye to a friend who is moving far away. You might feel sad, but if they promised to always stay connected, it would make you feel better. That's what happened when Jesus ascended into heaven. His disciples watched as He rose into the sky, but before He left, He made a promise—He would always be with them through the Holy Spirit.

Even though we can't see Jesus with our eyes, He is still with us every day. Through the Holy Spirit, He guides, comforts, and strengthens us.

He didn't leave us alone—He gave us everything we need to live for Him!

🚀 Think About It:

🟦 How can you remember that Jesus is always with you?

🟦 What does it mean to live with the power of the Holy Spirit?

⬤ Challenge: Trust in Jesus' Presence

When you feel alone or afraid, pray and remember that Jesus is always near.

🙏 Prayer: Thank You for Always Being With Me

Dear Jesus,

Even though I can't see You, I know You are always with me. Thank You for sending the Holy Spirit to help and guide me. Help me to trust You every day and to live boldly for You. Amen.

Conclusion

What Have We Learned? (A Quick Recap of the Journey)

Over the past 40 days, we have walked through Jesus' life, His sacrifice, and His victory. We started by preparing our hearts for Lent, learning about repentance, prayer, fasting, and trusting God. We then explored what it means to follow Jesus, serve others, forgive, and love the way He does. We faced Jesus' journey to the cross, His suffering, and ultimately His glorious resurrection on Easter morning!

But Lent and Easter are not just events we remember once a year. They are an invitation to live differently every day. Jesus' love, sacrifice, and resurrection give us hope, freedom, and a new life in Him. Now that we've completed this journey, the question remains: How will we continue to follow Jesus every day?

📌 How Can I Follow Jesus Every Day?

Following Jesus doesn't end with Easter—it's the beginning of a lifelong adventure with Him! Here are some simple ways to keep growing in faith every day:

✔ Spend Time with God – Read your Bible, pray, and listen to His voice daily.

✔ Live with Love and Kindness – Treat others the way Jesus did—with kindness, forgiveness, and compassion.

✔ Stay Connected to a Faith Community – Go to church, youth group, or Bible study to keep learning and growing.

✔ Share Your Faith – Tell others about Jesus through your words, actions, and the way you live.

✔ Trust Jesus in Hard Times – Even when life is tough, remember that Jesus is with you and will guide you through.

Following Jesus is not about being perfect—it's about walking with Him daily, trusting in His love, and growing in faith!

📌 A Special Easter Prayer

Dear Jesus,

Thank You for leading me on this journey of Lent and Easter. I have learned so much about Your love, sacrifice, and resurrection. Help me to keep following You, not just today, but every day of my life. Strengthen my faith, guide my steps, and fill my heart with Your love. May I always remember that You are with me, and may I share Your light with those around me. Thank You for dying for me, rising again, and giving me the gift of eternal life. I love You, Jesus! Amen.

📌 Fun Activities

🌸 Memory Verses

Here are some special verses to remember as you continue your journey with Jesus:

📖 John 3:16 – *"For God so loved the world that He gave His one and only Son, that whoever believes in Him shall not perish but have eternal life."*

📖 Romans 10:9 - "If you declare with your mouth, 'Jesus is Lord,' and believe in your heart that God raised Him from the dead, you will be saved."

📖 Matthew 28:6 - "He is not here; He has risen, just as He said!"

✏ Coloring Pages

Enjoy these fun coloring pages that remind you of the Easter story! Color pictures of Jesus, the cross, the empty tomb, and joyful celebrations of His resurrection!

🔎 Word Search

Find hidden words like Resurrection, Cross, Disciples, Faith, Hope, Love, Easter, and Jesus in this fun Easter word search!

🎉 Final Thought: Keep the Joy of Easter in Your Heart!

Easter is not just a day—it's a celebration of Jesus' victory that lasts forever! Keep growing in faith, sharing His love, and walking with Him every day. Jesus is alive, and He is with you always!

Made in the USA
Monee, IL
02 March 2025

13236331R00059